An Insider's Guide to
BASEBALL

GLEN F. STANLEY AND JASON PORTERFIELD

rosen publishing's
rosen central®

NEW YORK

Published in 2015 by The Rosen Publishing Group, Inc.
29 East 21st Street, New York, NY 10010

Copyright © 2015 by The Rosen Publishing Group, Inc.

First Edition

Library of Congress Cataloging-in-Publication Data

Stanley, Glen F.
An insider's guide to baseball/Glen F. Stanley and Jason Porterfield.
  pages cm. -- (Sports tips, techniques, and strategies)
Includes bibliographical references and index.
ISBN 978-1-4777-8577-5 (library bound)—ISBN 978-1-4777-8578-2 (pbk.)—
ISBN 978-1-4777-8580-5 (6-pack)
1. Baseball. I. Porterfield, Jason. II. Title.
GV867.S76 2015
796.357—dc23

                                                                    2013043298

Manufactured in Malaysia

Metric Conversion Chart			
1 inch	2.54 centimeters 25.4 millimeters	1 cup	250 milliliters
1 foot	30.48 centimeters	1 ounce	28 grams
1 yard	.914 meters	1 fluid ounce	30 milliliters
1 square foot	.093 square meters	1 teaspoon	5 milliliters
1 square mile	2.59 square kilometers	1 tablespoon	15 milliliters
1 ton	.907 metric tons	1 quart	.946 liters
1 pound	454 grams	355 degrees F	180 degrees C
1 mile	1.609 kilometers		

Contents

CHAPTER 1

The History of Baseball

Among the various team sports played in the United States, baseball is the oldest and most popular. Since its early development in the late 1830s, the sport has undergone many changes. However, it still remains connected to its earliest traditions. Baseball has evolved from children's recreation to a spectator sport appreciated by millions. Today, baseball's broad appeal has brought the game to people around the world, particularly in Canada, Japan, and Latin America.

Origins of Baseball

America's national pastime is not a completely original concept. The ancient Greeks, Persians, and Egyptians all played stick-and-ball games, recreationally and for ceremonial purposes. These games were not much like modern baseball, apart from the focus on hitting a ball with a stick. Variations of these games had spread to Europe by the Middle Ages.

Baseball was a popular sport for children in the Seattle City Light company town of Newhalem, Washington, in 1954.

Baseball's origin is probably one such game called rounders, which was brought to America by English settlers during the 1700s. In rounders, a player had to hit a ball that had been pitched to him and run around the bases without being called out. There were many local variations of rounders, and nearly as many names for the game, including town ball, one o'cat, four o'cat, goal ball, and baste ball.

Up until the 1800s, rounders and all of its forms were considered children's games. For adults, only gentlemen with leisure time played games, usually at gentlemen's clubs. However, as the 1800s progressed, rounders and its variations became increasingly popular with adults. Teams regularly formed at colleges and at military forts and bases, where men had ample time for recreation. Towns and villages sometimes formed teams for special events. Problems arose, however, when teams from different places played against each other. Rounders had no set rules, so different teams often played according to different conventions.

Alexander Cartwright and Abner Doubleday

According to legend, baseball was invented in Cooperstown, New York, in 1839. A popular story tells of how a young soldier named Abner Doubleday laid out a baseball diamond in a cow pasture, writing down rules and the proper dimensions of the field. Since Doubleday denied the story later, we're still unsure of the true origins of the baseball diamond.

Abner Doubleday, above, was a major general in the American Civil War. He was regarded by some as the inventor of baseball, but historians doubt this fact.

However, we do know that in 1845, Alexander Cartwright published the first book of baseball rules. Called *The Knickerbocker Rules*, it formed the basis for the rules of modern baseball. Cartwright's rules were widely adopted, and by 1866, teams had formed from Oregon to Maine.

At first, baseball was strictly an amateur sport. However, teams soon began paying their better players to participate. In 1869, the Cincinnati team became the first wholly professional baseball team. An organization of professional teams called the National League formed in 1876, becoming the first true major league.

Alexander Cartwright, apart from formalizing the first set of baseball rules, also founded the Knickerbocker Baseball Club.

Other leagues formed to compete with the National League, but most failed within a few years. It wasn't until the formation of the American League, in 1901, that the National League had a worthy rival. In 1903, the best team in each league, the Pittsburgh Pirates of the National League and the Boston Americans of the American League, played against each other in the first World Series. It was a best-of-nine series that Boston won, five games to three.

The Evolution of Baseball

During the 1880s and 1890s, baseball was a high-scoring game. Around the turn of the century, however, pitchers became more dominant, and scores dropped. Pitchers at this time had an advantage because the same baseballs were used throughout a game, so the balls became softer and more difficult to hit hard. Instead of relying on power hitting, the offense concentrated on speed and strategy. Bunts, stolen bases, and plays like the hit-and-run were very valuable for teams to score runs.

But the game changed again due to a couple of rule changes. First, beginning in 1920, it became illegal for pitchers to cut or scuff the ball. Then, a new rule required umpires to change baseballs throughout the course of a game. Under these rules, pitchers no longer dominated. Once the emphasis shifted to power hitting and driving in runs, home run hitters like Babe Ruth were the new stars of baseball.

In the early 1900s, the rules of baseball began to change. This changed the game radically. Shown above is an artist's depiction of the early game.

Babe Ruth—The Legend

George Herman "Babe" Ruth (1895-1948) began his career with the Boston Red Sox as a successful pitcher. At the suggestion of a teammate, Ruth was moved to the outfield and given a chance to be an everyday player. In 1919, he set a new single-season record by hitting twenty-nine home runs. The Red Sox sold his contract to the New York Yankees at the end of the season, and Ruth went on to become one of the greatest home run hitters of all time. He broke his own record by hitting fifty-four home runs in 1920. Ruth's exploits on the field brought in many new fans to baseball. Hitters imitated his big swing, making home runs more common. During his career in New York, Ruth played in seven World Series championships and helped the team win four. In 1935 he retired with 714 home runs, a record that would still be standing had Hank Aaron not surpassed it in 1974.

This statue of Babe Ruth, at the Oriole Park at Camden Yards in Baltimore, Maryland, USA, was placed there on his 100th birthday in February, 1995.

Formation of New Leagues: The Negro Leagues

African Americans were not allowed to play major league baseball by the National League and the American League until the late 1940s. However, teams made up exclusively of African Americans were common. The first all-black professional team, the Trenton Cuban Giants, played their first season in 1885. Eventually, all-black teams formed their own organizations, known collectively as the Negro Leagues.

Between 1938 and 1947, the best teams from the Negro National League and the Negro American League played in their own annual World Series, similar to the all-white leagues. Many outstanding players, including pitcher Satchel Paige, catcher Josh Gibson, and the speedy outfielder James "Cool Papa" Bell competed in the Negro Leagues.

Leroy Robert "Satchel" Paige was elected to the Baseball Hall of Fame in 1971.

Josh Gibson served as the first manager of the Santurce Crabbers, one of the most historic franchises of the Puerto Rico Baseball League.

Andrew Foster was an African-American pitcher who founded and managed the Chicago American Giants.

Inclusion of African Americans

Brooklyn Dodgers' general manager Branch Rickey offered a contract to a Negro League player named Jackie Robinson in 1945, ending the segregation of African Americans. When the 1947 season began, many fans and other players were outraged to see a black man playing for a major league team. Robinson took a great deal of abuse both on and off the field, but he maintained his focus and dignity throughout the season. Rickey and especially the Dodgers' shortstop, Pee Wee Reese, continually voiced their support for Robinson, who quietly won over the fans with his patience and his skill.

Jackie Robinson was the first African American to be inducted into the Baseball Hall of Fame in 1962. Shown above is a stamp released in his honor.

When the season ended, the Dodgers had won the National League pennant, and Jackie Robinson was voted the major league Rookie of the Year. Robinson played for the Dodgers until he retired in 1956, winning the National League's Most Valuable Player award in 1949 and helping his team win the 1955 World Series.

Other managers, impressed by Robinson's success, began signing African American players. In 1948, Larry Doby of the Cleveland Indians became the first African American to play in the American League. By 1950, three other teams had integrated, and by 1958, one year after the Negro Leagues collapsed, all sixteen major league teams had at least one African American player in the team.

A statue of Jackie Robinson and
Pee Wee Reese stands tall in New York.

Current Baseball

Even today, baseball is played in much the same way as it was played in the 1920s, although the face of the Major League Baseball has changed significantly. Hispanic players from Mexico, South America, and the Caribbean began appearing on major league rosters in the 1960s. And at the beginning of the 21st century, players from East Asian countries such as Japan and South Korea were having an impact on Major League Baseball. For example, Ichiro Suzuki, outfielder for the New York Yankees, is one of the most promising players today, and he hails from Japan.

As the popularity of the sport spreads, people from all over the world are making a name for themselves in Major League Baseball.

Spread across twenty-eight teams in the United States, and one—the Toronto Blue Jays—in Canada, there are now roughly 900 major league baseball players. In addition, thousands of minor league, high school, and college players compete against each other annually. Around the world, thousands of Little League teams play every summer.

Even though no major league team has signed a woman yet,
a lot more are playing little league baseball.

As of 2013, no major league team had signed a woman to a contract, but that may change in the coming years. More girls are playing little league than ever before, and some are choosing to play baseball in high school instead of softball, the traditional women's alternative. The amateur-level American Women's Baseball Federation formed in 1992 to coordinate women's baseball tournaments and promote the sport among women and girls. Between 2001 and 2004, the organization put together four Women's World Series events, with participants from the national teams of United States, Japan, Canada, and other countries.

CHAPTER 2

Player Positions and the Baseball Field

The two areas that make up the baseball field are the infield and the outfield. Most of the action during a game takes place in the infield, a diamond-shaped area with a base at each corner. The infield's boundaries are formed by the base paths for first and third base and the grass line marking the beginning of the outfield.

Home plate, the bottom point of the baseball diamond, is the main focus of play during a game. On either side of home plate are the batter's boxes, six-foot by three-foot rectangles painted in the dirt, where the batter stands and waits for the pitch. A fence called a backstop prevents any loose balls or wild pitches from leaving the field behind home plate. At the top of a raised mound in the middle of the infield is the pitching rubber, from which the pitcher throws the ball. The rubber is officially located 60.5 feet from home plate. Major league rules state that the top of the pitching rubber may be no more than ten inches higher than home plate.

Going counterclockwise from home plate is first base, succeeded by second and third. From third base, a base runner returns to home plate. The base paths are all the same length, 90 feet from one base to the next. First, second, and third bases are all slightly raised square cushions, while home plate is a pentagonal rubber slab set into the ground.

Players waiting to bat or take the field sit on benches along the first-and third-baselines. Often, these benches are placed inside an area called a dugout. Dugouts may be as simple as a roofless enclosure made up of chain-link fencing, or they may be solidly built structures of cinderblocks and concrete. Traditionally, the home team takes the dugout along the first-base line. Pitchers warm up on a special area in the field, called a bullpen, before entering a game.

Shown above is the typical layout of a baseball pitch.

The Catcher and the Pitcher

A pitcher throws the ball, hoping to strike out the batter.

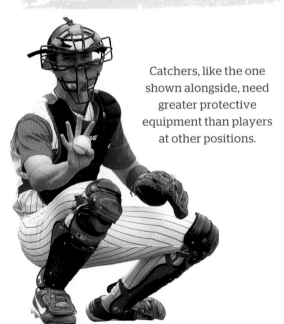

Catchers, like the one shown alongside, need greater protective equipment than players at other positions.

The pitcher throws the ball toward the home plate for batters to try and hit it, which makes them the starting point of all the action in a baseball game. Pitchers also make plays on balls hit near the mound and try to keep base runners from advancing. There are two types of pitchers: starters and relievers.

The pitchers with the most stamina are generally starters. When the starter gets tired or pitches poorly, a relief pitcher comes. In youth leagues, the starter often pitches the whole game. However, in major league baseball, the starter usually lasts for six or seven innings. After that, a middle reliever pitches for an inning or two, and then another reliever—the closer—pitches the last inning or two to finish the game.

On defense, catchers have the most demanding job on the field. They crouch behind the plate on every pitch, catching the ball and returning it to the pitcher. They also use hand signals to indicate to the pitcher which pitch to throw and where. This is called "calling" the game. In addition, catchers try to throw out runners stealing bases and tag out runners trying to score.

The catcher is the most heavily armored player on the field, wearing a helmet, a face mask with a throat guard, an athletic cup, shin guards, a bulky glove with extra padding, and a chest protector. All of this gear protects the catcher from errant pitches, foul tips, and also during the occasional collision with a base runner trying to make it to home plate.

What's a No-Hitter?

One of the most impressive pitching feats is throwing a no-hitter. This is a game in which the opposing team fails to get a single hit. For most pitchers, throwing a no-hitter is a once-in-a-lifetime event, though some major league players accomplished the feat multiple times. Hall of Famer Nolan Ryan holds the record, having pitched seven no-hitters. A pitcher may allow walks during a no-hitter, and the team that fails to get a hit may even score runs. For example, in 1964, Ken Johnson of the Houston Astros pitched a no-hitter but still lost the game against the Cincinnati Reds because of a run scored on an error!

Nolan Ryan, shown to the right, holds the record for no-hitters.

(continued on page 18)

(continued from page 17)

Pitching a perfect game is a rare achievement. There are no-hitters in which the pitcher retires all twenty-seven batters in a row, with no walks or errors. Since 1903, there have been only twenty-one perfect games pitched in the major leagues. The last occurred in 2012, when Félix Hernández of the Seattle Mariners Diamondbacks pitched a perfect game against the Tampa Bay Rays.

Cy Young, shown here, holds the Major League record for most complete games.

Brandon Shaves, the Bridgeport Bluefish infielder, stands safely at second base after hitting a double.

Playing Defense: On the Field

Defense players are either infielders or outfielders. Individual positions come with their own special responsibilities, but the best teams are often the ones that work together seamlessly and play the best team defense.

Each of the bases is defended by a fielder. The first baseman guards the area around first base. The second baseman covers second base and most of the territory between first and second. The third baseman covers the area around third. The position between second base and third base is taken by the shortstop, who also fields the entire surrounding area. Because they must cover so much territory, shortstops are usually the quickest, most nimble players on a team. Typically, shortstops and second basemen are more agile than the first and third basemen, since they must cover areas both to their right and left and make throws from difficult angles.

The outfield is covered by the right fielder, the left fielder, and the center fielder. The outfield technically includes all of the area beyond the base paths, although infielders usually make plays on balls hit between the base paths and the outfield grass line. Any grounders, line drives, or fly balls hit beyond the infield become the responsibility of the outfielders.

Outfielders must be fast and coordinated. A strong, accurate throwing arm is also a desired trait. Of the three outfielders, the center fielder has the most territory to cover, and so he is usually the fastest and most athletic.

Foul lines extending from home plate along the base paths to first and third and beyond mark the side boundaries of the outfield. The area outside this line is called foul territory. Usually, the farthest boundary of the outfield is marked by a curved wall or fence. If a fly ball lands beyond this boundary, it is a home run.

Cal Ripken Jr. is a legendary shortstop. He played 2,632 consecutive games.

Playing Offense: Batting Order and Batters

All those who play on the field get a chance to bat. Team managers carefully consider the order in which their players come to bat. The batting order cannot be changed in the middle of the game, so the best hitters usually bat in the first few spots in the lineup. This way, they have more chances to get on base.

Aaron Hicks swings at a pitch during the Eastern League baseball game in Trenton, NJ, 2012.

The first spot in the batting order, the leadoff position, usually goes to the fastest and most alert base runner. The second and third positions generally go to good hitters who also are speedy on the base paths. The fourth, or cleanup, batter is usually the most powerful hitter on the team, with a proven ability to drive in runs. The weaker hitters on the team often play at the bottom slots.

Coaches and Managers

The responsibilities of a baseball manager include drawing the lineup card, making substitutions during a game, and planning a team's strategy. In professional baseball, the manager is assisted by a team of specialized coaches, who focus on such areas as batting and pitching. Little league and youth league managers usually act as both pitching and hitting coaches, although volunteers or former players may help out.

Shown above is the former Los Angeles Dodgers manager, Tommy Lasorda, during the Major League Baseball game on Sept. 22, 2011, at Dodger Stadium in Los Angeles, CA.

During the game, the hitting team is aided by base coaches at first base and third base. These coaches keep their eyes on the action on the field and direct the runners, telling them whether to hold up at the base or advance to the next one. Other players often act as base coaches in youth league games.

Arizona Diamondbacks coach, Bo Porter, is throwing in batting practice prior to a game on July 28, 2010, in Philadelphia.

Protective Gear and Uniforms

An identical uniform is worn by all players and coaches on a team, usually made up of a cap, jersey, and cotton pants. On their feet, players wear cleats, shoes with hard nubs or spikes on the soles designed to give them traction on the base paths. Outfielders sometimes have to look up to field fly balls, so they'll usually wear sunglasses during day games. Batters may wear batting gloves to help them keep their grip on the bat and to protect their hands when they slide into bases.

All members of a team wear the same uniform.
The Richmond Spiders (shown above) wear blue jerseys.

School teams must also wear uniforms
and protective gear while playing.

Since most of the baseball season is played in the summer, jerseys are generally short-sleeved. Some teams also have long-sleeved jerseys for colder weather. Professional, college, and high school teams have two different uniforms, one for home games and one for away games.

Baseball is not a game that requires a lot of protective gear, unlike football or hockey.

Most players do not wear any special protection when playing the field, although male players usually wear a hard plastic athletic cup to protect the groin region. Batters wear helmets to protect themselves from stray pitches, and some batters also wear special pads to protect elbows, forearms, shins, and the tops of their front foot.

The Equipment

Baseball equipment is usually standardized to meet specific rules. Fielder's gloves are usually made of stiff leather. The dominant feature of a baseball glove is the basket, the flexible material between the thumb and forefinger where fielders trap most balls when making a play. Players who throw right-handed wear their gloves on their left hand so that their throwing arm is free. The reverse is true for left-handed players.

Baseball equipment includes the baseball glove, bats, and of course, the ball.

Baseballs are about nine inches in circumference. The baseball's core is made of cork or rubber wrapped in layers of synthetic string and rubber and covered with stitched rawhide. Game balls are white with red stitching.

In the major leagues, bats cannot be longer than 42 inches. The bat tapers from the barrel to the narrower grip. The barrel must be less than 2.75 inches in diameter. In the major leagues, bats are made of wood, traditionally ash or maple. In Little League games, batters are allowed to use bats made of aluminum, which doesn't break like wood. Aluminum bats are also lighter, meaning that players swing them faster, generating faster bat speeds and more power. This additional power would give professional batters an unnecessary advantage, so aluminum bats are not allowed in the major leagues. Additionally, baseball purists prefer wooden bats. The "crack" produced by a wooden bat satisfies them far more than the "ding" sound an aluminum bat makes.

CHAPTER 3

The Game

There are nine periods of play, called innings, over which a baseball game is played. The team that scores more runs over the course of those nine innings wins the game. Each inning is divided into two parts, the top and the bottom. The visiting team bats in the top of the inning, while the home team bats in the bottom. The team batting is allowed three outs per inning. After three outs, the other team comes to bat.

Batter's Offensive Strategy

Right-handed hitters, like the one shown above, turn to the left while hitting. Left-handed hitters stand on the other side and turn to the right.

The batter's first goal is to get safely on base, preferably by hitting a pitch. The best hitters have excellent eye-hand coordination and can hit a ball where there is no fielder to catch it. Once the ball is in play, fielders attempt to make plays to prevent the hitting team from scoring runs. A play ends when the runners on the bases have been called safe out and the ball is returned to the pitcher.

At the start of a play, the batter stands in the batter's box, ready for the pitch. The batter may swing at the pitch if it is hittable.

The batter also has the option of not swinging or "taking" the pitch. If the batter takes a pitch and it passes through the strike zone, the umpire calls the pitch a "strike." (The strike zone is an imaginary space directly over home plate and between the batter's knees and armpits.) If the pitch passes outside the strike zone—whether too high, too low, or off the inside or outside of the plate—the umpire calls the pitch a "ball." Patient batters will take four balls and advance to first base with a "walk." In many situations, a walk is as good as a hit; it helps to tire out the pitcher, too.

If the batter swings at a pitch and misses, it is a strike. It is also a strike if the batter swings and makes contact but the ball strays into foul territory. The batter is allowed three strikes or four balls to put the ball in play. If the pitcher throws three strikes past the batter, it is an out—a strikeout. If a batter has two strikes and hits a swinging foul ball, however, he continues to bat.

When a batter makes contact and the ball lands between the foul lines, the ball is considered "fair," and the batter must run to first base while fielders attempt to make a play. After hitting the ball, the batter advances to the farthest possible base. A single is a hit on which the batter safely advances to first base; on a double, the batter makes it to second base; on a triple, the batter reaches third. The home run is the most desirable run. This occurs if a batter makes it all the way back home to score his own hit.

This player is diving to make it safely to third base.

Baserunning

One of the most crucial aspects of the game is baserunning. The batter becomes a base runner after safely reaching base. In order to score a run, the runner must advance safely to each base and come back to home.

A player tries to avoid being tagged out between first and second base.

Since only one runner is allowed on a base at a time, if the batter puts the ball in play or walks, a runner standing on first must advance to second. However, if a runner is on second or third and the previous base is empty, the runner is not forced to advance. If there are less than two out and a ball in the air is caught, a base runner may try to advance to the next base, but only after the catch is made.

Base runners must remain alert and know where the ball is at all times. They seldom stand touching the base during another player's at-bat. Instead, they take a "lead," standing a few feet off base, ready to run if the batter makes contact. Speedy base runners may also try to advance to an open base during a pitcher's windup and delivery. This is called attempting to "steal" a base. Runners planning to steal often take a big lead off, making their intentions clear. Instead of winding up and throwing to the plate, an alert pitcher may try to throw to a base to "pick off" the runner. If a fielder tags the runner before he is able to return to the base, the runner is out. If the runner attempts to break for the next base during the pitcher's throw toward home plate, the catcher steps in. The catcher then throws to the base being stolen and the fielder tries to tag the runner out.

A runner with good technique can get around the bases quickly. When running from home to first on an infield ground ball, a runner should "run through" first base, since he can't be tagged out in that situation. If a batter hits a ball through the infield, he should immediately be thinking of trying for a double. If the outfielder bobbles the ball, he will have a better chance of getting making it to second base.

Between bases, the runner should travel in as straight a line as possible, listening to a coach's instructions or stopping at the next base and locating the ball quickly. When approaching a base, runners looking to advance further should begin their turn as they approach the base. Then they round the base, stepping on an inside corner as they pass.

If the situation calls for the runner to run hard into a base, sliding is a good way to avoid getting tagged out. The safest slides are made feet-first. Putting a hand down while sliding may cause hand and wrist injuries, which is why it is best if it is avoided by runners.

A neat slide towards the home plate helps this player complete a run.

The Sacrifice Bunt: Offensive Strategy

In baseball, the difference between winning and losing may just be a single run. For this reason, a manager may call for a batter to "sacrifice bunt." For this play, a hitter surrenders his chance to get on base in the interest of moving a teammate forward to second or third base. To execute a sacrifice bunt, the batter holds the bat directly across the plate with one hand on the handle and the other further down the barrel. Instead of swinging hard at the pitch, the batter tries to make soft contact, hitting the ball on the ground a few feet away from the plate. Since a fielder has to run in from his position, a base runner will usually have time to advance to the next base on a sacrifice bunt. The batter, however, is usually thrown out at first base.

Richmond batter Matt Zink bunts during a game in Camden, NJ, 2011.

Pitching: Defensive Strategy

At the heart of a baseball game is the battle between the batter and the pitcher. A successful pitcher uses a combination of different pitches and pitch locations to either strike the batter out or force him to hit balls he would prefer not to hit.

There are many different pitches used in baseball. The ball will act differently depending on how the pitcher grips the ball, the motion of the wrist as it is released, and the speed at which it is thrown. The change-up, the fastball, the knuckleball, the curveball, and the split-finger are some common pitches.

A player throws a pitch.
Pitches can be of different kinds.

Pitchers rock back and "wind up" for the pitch to generate as much power as possible. Although arm strength is important for a pitcher, it is through lower body strength that a pitcher creates momentum to throw fastballs. A high kick and a good push off the rubber allow a hard-throwing pitcher to avoid strains and injuries to his elbow and shoulder. Durable pitchers also follow through properly after releasing the pitch, bending forward to the opposite side of the body from the throwing arm, ending with the armpit just over the knee.

The Numbers Tell the Story

The real history of baseball is told in numerical records called statistics. They allow fans to compare players from different eras.

For pitchers, the important statistics are traditionally the earned-run average (E.R.A.), games won, and strikeouts recorded. E.R.A. represents the average number of earned runs allowed by a pitcher per nine innings pitched. In 1968, St. Louis Cardinal pitcher Bob Gibson recorded the lowest E.R.A. in major league history for a pitcher throwing at least 300 innings. That year, his E.R.A. was an amazing 1.12.

Nolan Ryan holds the modern record for most strikeouts in a season by a pitcher. In 1973, he struck out 383 batters.

Bob Gilson holds the record for the lowest E.R.A. in major league history.

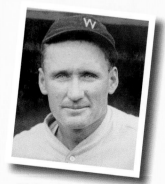

Walter Johnson won more than thirty games in consecutive seasons.

(continued on page 32)

(continued from page 31)

A twenty-win season is a major pitching achievement today. In the early 1900s, Walter Johnson and Cy Young both won more than thirty games in consecutive seasons!

Hitters have their own statistics, too. The most telling hitting statistic is a player's batting average. This number indicates the proportion of times a batter gets a hit to reach base safely. A batting average of .300 is considered pretty good in the major leagues. The highest average ever by a major-league player in a single season was .424. Rogers Hornsby recorded this average in 1924, playing for the Saint Louis Cardinals. No batter has hit better than .400 since Ted Williams hit .406 in 1941. The highest career average in major league history is .367. Ty Cobb, in a career spanning from 1905 to 1928, achieved this feat.

Ted Williams was also a World War II and Korean War veteran.

Cy Young pitched for five different teams.

Fielding: Defensive Strategy

As the batting team tries to bring runners around to score, the fielders try to get them out before they can accomplish their goal. There are several ways in which fielders make outs. If the ball is hit in the air, they can catch it for an out. If the ball is hit on the ground, they can catch the ball and tag the runner with it, or they can step on a base ahead of the runner while in possession of the ball. This last play is called a "force out" and it occurs if there is another runner on the base directly behind the one the runner is on, "forcing" him to advance.

The fielder must throw the ball to the infielder most likely to make an out, if he has the ball in hand and cannot tag the runner himself. When infielders get two runners out on the same play, it is called a double play. Double plays are rather common. For the rare triple play, the fielders get three runners out on the same play.

If a fielder botches a play or a throw and the runner is safe, it is called an error. To avoid errors, a fielder uses good technique. To catch a fly ball or pop-up, he runs quickly to get under the ball and secures it in the glove using his bare hand. With ground balls, fielders should kneel or get close to the ground directly in front of the ball. Their eyes should always remain on the ball as it rolls or hops into the glove.

The infielder dives to catch the ball in an attempt to get a batter out.

Enforcing the Rules

The rules in baseball rarely change. When they do, they are added to the official rule book, a document studied by all umpires, managers, and coaches. On the field, the umpires (umps) enforce the rules. In the pros, there are at least three umps on the field for regular games. The ump behind home plate wears a face mask and chest protector in case of foul balls or wild pitches. The two other umps take up positions by first base and third. In Little League and youth league games, there are usually only two umpires, one behind the plate and one in the field.

Umpires make the call on whether a pitch is a ball or a strike, whether a ball lands fair or foul, and whether a runner is safe or out. They have the right to check bats and balls for illegal modifications. Umpires may also eject players and managers from a game for arguing or breaking the rules. If an umpire does his or her job well, the game runs smoothly. "The best umpires are the ones you never notice." This old baseball saying possibly sums it up best.

Shown above is the National League baseball
umpire Bob Emslie in 1914.

CHAPTER 4

Preparing for the Game

A baseball team comprises of players that possess different skills. The best pitchers are rarely the best hitters, the fastest runners are not necessarily the best fielders, and the most powerful sluggers may strike out more than anyone on the team. Every team has room for a player who is willing to work to improve. Like most team athletes, baseball players must work hard to keep in shape, improve their knowledge of the game, and maintain their form.

Warm-up and Stretching

Playing baseball requires coordination, flexibility, speed, and strength. Before games and practice, players usually spend twenty minutes to an hour stretching their muscles and warming up to avoid injuries. Commonly, pre-game warm-up exercises are light, usually a jog around the field before stretching. It is important to be in good physical condition for a wide range of activities before joining a team. Before the season begins, many players do weight training and run to get into shape.

Professional players do a lot of weight training, especially just before the season begins.

Steroids in Baseball

A good way for professional ball players to stay in shape for the long season is weight training. However, most physicians recommend that young athletes do not start serious weight training until they are at least fifteen or sixteen years old. Rapidly growing bodies of younger athletes are much more likely to suffer torn ligaments and muscles from weight lifting.

Recently, the issues of steroids and other performance enhancing drugs have received a lot of attention in the media. Cheaters use steroids to become stronger and faster. However, studies have related steroid use to severe health problems, including premature heart attacks, strokes, liver tumors, kidney failure, and serious psychiatric problems. It goes without saying that players at all levels should avoid steroids.

Not only are there physical dangers to using steroids, but you may also lose the privilege of playing on a team. Minor league teams have very strict policies forbidding drug use, as do many high school and college programs. In most cases, the steroid user is suspended from the team for several games after the first offence and banned after the second. MLB began testing for steroids only in 2003, though evidence indicating that steroid use has been a problem in Major League Baseball as far back as the early 1900s has been found.

Using steroids to boost one's play is a problem that MLB has been facing for a long time now.

Fundamental Skills and Drills

The focus at practice is often on drills, where the same activity is practiced over and over again, until the motions become second nature for the players. Pitchers work with catchers on their control, concentrating on placing the ball over particular parts of home plate. They may also try different pitches in practice, or they may experiment with changing the way they throw a particular pitch to get better results.

For their part, outfielders "shag" fly balls and work on making strong, accurate throws to the right base. Infielders scoop up grounder after grounder and work on their footwork and throwing form. They also work on catching infield pop-ups, calling "Mine!" or "I got it!" to let their teammates know to stay out of the way.

Batters work on their swing, and they practice hitting pitches that give them trouble. They also work on bunting technique. Base runners may practice running technique, getting a good lead off, stealing bases, and sliding to avoid tags.

Practice may also include other running drills and weight training. For all athletes, strong core muscles (abdominal and back muscles) are important to performing well. For hitters, strong forearms are the key to bat control. To develop these muscles, you can ask your coach for specific exercises.

Crunches help develop the abdominal muscles,
while weights help develop biceps and forearms.

Baseball Seasons

The length of a baseball season differs from league to league. For Little League and other youth league players, practices begin in mid- to late spring, with the season played out over the summer months. One or two games are typically played per week.

The Akron Aeros celebrate winning the Eastern League baseball championship on the field on September 15, 2012, in Trenton, NJ.

The team with the best record is usually awarded the youth league championship, though sometimes the top teams compete in a playoff game. In high school and college baseball, the best two teams in a district or athletic conference compete in a championship game, with the winner taking home the district trophy. The winning team may move on to regional competition and even advance as far as a state or national championship game.

Major league teams play 162 games, with the season beginning in April and ending during the third week of September. The first round of the playoffs begin soon after, with the winners advancing to the league championship series, a seven-game playoff. The league champions advance to the World Series, which starts the last week of October. The winner of the best-of-seven World Series is declared world champ.

Beginning to Play

If you would like to play in the World Series some day, you have to start playing. Getting involved in baseball is easy, as many towns have leagues for all age groups. Signing up for Little League is usually as simple as showing up for the first practice. In some larger communities with multiple teams, there may be tryouts and a player draft, in which managers from each team select new players, one by one. Many locales also have leagues for players too old for Little League; inquire at your local community center if you would like to play. Players who are interested in joining a junior high

Children interested in playing baseball join Little Leagues.

or a middle school team often try out to earn a place on the team. Those looking to improve their skills in the off-season may attend baseball camps, often run by former professional players. Older players usually have to try out for high school or college teams. Adults may play in town or neighborhood leagues.

Community, or municipal, leagues often sponsored by local businesses, are generally open to anyone within the age requirement. The teams usually provide uniforms, balls, helmets, and often bats. Players themselves usually have to bring their own gloves and cleats.

Even if there are no formal leagues nearby, you can always form a team of your own with friends and neighbors, improvising your own rules to fit your situation. Many such games are played in backyards and parks every day, often with just a handful of people, a ball, and a bat. A day at a baseball camp, whether you play or simply watch, is a great experience. It helps form a connection to a long tradition of a game that is a part of life in the United States.

Glossary

battery In baseball lingo, a team's pitching and catching unit.

batting average A personal statistic indicating the percentage of times a batter gets a hit. Batting average is arrived at by dividing the number of hits by the number of at bats.

bunt To hit a baseball lightly, without swinging the bat.

draft A selection process in which teams take turns claiming players from a common pool.

earned-run average (E.R.A.) A personal statistic for pitchers. It indicates the average number of earned runs a pitcher allows per nine innings.

fly ball A hit that flies into the air.

grounder A hit that rolls and bounces along the ground.

inning In a baseball game, a period of play during which each teams get a turn to bat; a full baseball game lasts nine innings.

integrate To make open to people of all racial and ethnic groups.

lineup A list of batters arranged according to the order in which they will bat.

pitcher The member of a baseball team who throws the ball for a batter to try to hit.

run batted in (R.B.I.) In baseball, a statistic indicating that a batter is credited with hitting a ball that allowed a runner or runners to score.

shag In baseball, to practice catching fly balls in the outfield.

statistics Numbers and data used to evaluate the performance of baseball players.

steroids Hormones that can be used topically, ingested, or injected to promote muscle growth.

synthetic Produced artificially.

umpire An official at a baseball game who oversees play.

windup The beginning of a pitcher's motion, prior to delivering the pitch.

For More Information

Baseball Digest
Century Publishing Company
990 Grove St., Evanston, IL 60201
(888) 244-1228
Web site: http://www.centurysports.net/baseball/

International Baseball Association
311 N. Robertson Blvd. Suite 820
Beverly Hills CA 90211
(805) 750-1822
Web site: http://www.internationalbaseballassociation.com

Junior Baseball Organization Inc.
P.O. Box 784
Sherwood, OR 97140
Web site: http://www.juniorbaseballorg.com

Little League International
Williamsport, PA 17701
(570) 326-1921
Web site: http://www.littleleague.org/

Louisville Slugger Museum
800 West Main Street
Louisville, KY 40202
(877) 775 8443
Web site: http://www.sluggermuseum.com/

Major League Baseball

The Office of the Commissioner of Baseball

245 Park Ave., 31st floor

New York, NY 10167

(212) 931-7800

Web site: http://www.mlb.com

National Baseball Hall of Fame

25 Main Street

Cooperstown, New York 13326

(888) 425-5633

Web site: http://www.baseballhalloffame.org

The Negro Leagues Baseball Museum

1616 East 18th Street

Kansas City, MO 64108

(816) 221-1920

Web site: http://www.nlbm.com

Web Sites

Due to the changing nature of Internet links, the Rosen Publishing Group, Inc., has developed an online list of Web sites related to the subject of this book. This site is updated regularly. Please use this link to access the list:

http://www.rosenlinks.com/STTS/Base

For Further Reading

American Baseball Coaches Association. *Practice Perfect Baseball*. Champaigne, IL: Human Kinetics, 2009.

Banner, Stuart. *The Baseball Trust: A History of Baseball's Antitrust Exemption*. New York, NY: 2013.

Hample, Zack. *The Baseball: Stunts, Scandals, and Secrets Beneath the Stitches*. New York, NY: Random House, 2011.

Jonah, Keri E. *Baseball Between the Numbers*. New York, NY: Basic Books, 2007.

Neft, David S., Neft, Michael L., Cohen, Richard M. *The Sports Encyclopedia: Baseball 2007*. New York, NY: St. Martin's Griffin.

Neyer, Rob. *Rob Neyer's Big Book of Baseball Legends: The Truth, the Lies, and Everything Else*. New York, NY: Touchstone, 2008.

Pisapia, Joe. *The Fantasy Baseball Black Book*. Amazon Digital Services, 2012.

Schwarz, Alan. *Once Upon a Game: Baseball's Greatest Memories*. New York, NY: Houghton Mifflin Harcourt, 2007.

Thompson, Eric. *Baseball's LOST Tradition: The Untold Story of Baseball's First Self-imposed Expansion - The 1961 - 1962 Seasons*. Raleigh, NC: Lighthouse Publishing of the Carolinas, 2013.

Turbo, Jason, and Michael Duca. *The Baseball Codes: Beanballs, Sign Stealing, and Bench-Clearing Brawls: The Unwritten Rules of America's Pastime*. New York, NY: Anchor Books, 2011.

Vecsey, George. *Baseball: A History of America's Favorite Game* (*Modern Library Chronicles*). New York, NY: Random House Inc., 2008.

Bibliography

Alexander, Charles. *Our Game: An American Baseball History*. New York, NY: Henry Holt and Company, 1991.

Frommer, Harvey. *Primitive Baseball: The First Quarter-Century of the National Pastime*. New York, NY: Atheneum, 1988.

Koppett, Leonard. *Koppett's Concise History of Major League Baseball*. New York, NY: Carroll and Graf Publishers, 2004.

Nemec, David. *The Rules of Baseball: An Anecdotal Look at the Rules of Baseball and How They Came To Be*. New York, NY: Lyons & Burford, 1994.

Okrent, Daniel. *Nine Innings*. New York, NY: Ticknor & Fields, 1985.

Seymour, Harold. *Baseball: The People's Game*. New York, NY: Oxford University Press, 1990.

Index

About the Authors

Glen F. Stanley is a writer who lives in upstate New York. A devoted sports fan, Stanley enjoys playing third base on an adult league baseball team.

Jason Porterfield is a writer and a researcher living in Chicago. While growing up in Virginia, Porterfield was an outfielder for his hometown Little League team, the Newport Cubs. He bats and throws left-handed. His cousin, the late Bob Porterfield, pitched in the major leagues from 1948 to 1959. In 1953, Bob led the American League in wins (22) and shutouts (9) as a pitcher for the Washington Senators.

Photo Credits